JANUARY 1

"Life is a beautiful song. Open your heart and rejoice in its melody. Once you are attuned to this song, you will find the Composer seated in the lotus of your heart."

DECEMBER 31

"The final Reality is silence."

THE MASTER SPEAKS:

INSPIRED SAYINGS OF **SRI SWAMI RAMA**

a perpetual calendar

Acknowledgments

We would like to thank the following people for their exceptional photographic contributions to the calendar:

Dr. Sanjoy Das for outstanding photographs of the Indian Himalayas, nature and wildlife,

Kamal for flower and nature images,

Wesley van Linda for flower and nature images,

Dr. Prakash Keshaviah for assorted photographs of Indian landscapes, nature, and culture,

Karen Kenyon for images of Tarkeshwar and Rishikesh,

William Sparacia for landscape and nature images, and

Connie Gage for assorted images of India.

We also express our appreciation to Connie Gage for designing the beautiful cover. Last but not least, we would like to thank Dr. Barbara Bova for compiling the quotations of Sri Swami Rama and Wesley Van Linda for designing the calendar.

cover design: Connie Gage
ISBN 978-81-88157-46-4
Printed at Thomson Press India Ltd., New Delhi, India
Distributed by: Lotus Press, PO Box 325, Twin Lakes, WI 53181 USA, www.lotuspress.com, 1-800-824-6396

Published by:
Himalayan Institute Hospital Trust, Swami Ram Nagar, P.O. Doiwala, Distt. Dehradun 248140, Uttarakhand, India. www.hihtindia.org, src@hihtindia.org

JANUARY 2

"Pray to the Lord of life in your heart to give you strength and wisdom, so that you can understand life from all perspectives."

DECEMBER 30

"The most ancient traveler in the universe is love."

JANUARY 3

"Now is part of eternity."

DECEMBER 29

"There is only one Reality without second and without space, time, or causation. We call it Love."

JANUARY 4

"A human being is perfect though still incomplete."

DECEMBER 28

"In samadhi you are one with the Reality."

JANUARY 5

"You are the architect of your life."

DECEMBER 27

*"Once the river has met the ocean,
there is no way of going back."*

JANUARY 6

"Approach your life whole-heartedly."

DECEMBER 26

*"A perfect human being is one who has attained
the state of samadhi."*

JANUARY 7

"You have the power to change your destiny."

DECEMBER 25

"Samadhi is beyond all joys."

JANUARY 8

*"If you take care of your present, the future will
be at your disposal."*

DECEMBER 24

"God to me is a real annihilating fire and indescribable grace."

JANUARY 9

"There is always hope, and you should live with that hope."

DECEMBER 23

"Walk alone but do not be lonely, for actually you are alone, which means all in One."

JANUARY 10

"It is said that faith can move mountains, and it does."

DECEMBER 22

*"There is only One Who exists beneath all
the forms of the world."*

JANUARY 11

"There is nothing like impossible."

DECEMBER 21

"The sun, the moon, the stars, and all the lights that you can imagine in the entire external world are but fragments of that one great Light that is within you."

JANUARY 12

*"If you learn the technique of how to live here and now,
then every moment will be filled with happiness."*

DECEMBER 20

*"The Lord dwells in me. I am a finite vessel, and
Infinity dwells within this finite vessel."*

JANUARY 13

*"Humans are not so much bodies with souls
as they are souls with bodies."*

DECEMBER 19

"Belief in God and the experience of the presence of God at every moment are two different things."

JANUARY 14

*"Deep down within you there is a center
called the kingdom of God."*

DECEMBER 18

"The best of knowledge comes through revelation, not through the mind. It is a flood of knowledge that overwhelms the whole being."

JANUARY 15

"God pervades all and is the Atman animating your soul, the life of your life."

DECEMBER 17

*"The mind goes through different states of waking,
dreaming, and sleeping; eternity remains ever awake."*

JANUARY 16

"God did not create the world; One manifested into many."

DECEMBER 16

"The subtlest realm of love is unfathomable by those who live through their minds."

JANUARY 17

"God is the source of all energies, the powerhouse of light, life, and love."

DECEMBER 15

*"The greatest of all churches and temples is
the living human being."*

JANUARY 18

"God's existence does not depend on our proofs."

DECEMBER 14

"Spiritual Truth does not need an external witness."

JANUARY 19

"Your greatest friend is within."

DECEMBER 13

"One who believes in God and surrenders to God attains freedom here and now."

JANUARY 20

"You are a shrine of the Lord of life."

DECEMBER 12

"When emotion is led by devotion it is called ecstasy."

JANUARY 21

"You are human and at the same time you are God, because God is within you."

DECEMBER 11

"Illumination is attained by devotion toward God."

JANUARY 22

"The best part of you is God."

DECEMBER 10

"When you are quiet, let your mantra turn into feeling and then let that feeling become a wave of bliss within you."

JANUARY 23

"Your essential nature is a limitless horizon."

DECEMBER 9

"Silence does not lie within the domain of your mind; silence lies beyond your mind."

JANUARY 24

*"What is unique in the human being is
the awareness of consciousness."*

DECEMBER 8

"The best of all knowledge, the greatest of all powers, comes from silence."

JANUARY 25

"The same Self that dwells within you dwells in everyone. That Self is the center of consciousness."

DECEMBER 7

"Start from a personal God, go to the God within, then to the universal God, and finally beyond."

JANUARY 26

"Self-confidence means having confidence in the real Self of all, the very source of life and light within you."

DECEMBER 6

"If God is everywhere, then He is also in you.
You simply have to realize it."

JANUARY 27

"Those who have realized the real Self are immortal."

DECEMBER 5

"If you are ready and you have a burning desire within, you can enlighten yourself in a second's time."

JANUARY 28

"In this tree of life there are two fruits: one that sustains your life in this world, and another that leads you to the Divine."

DECEMBER 4

"Your enlightenment is not in the hands of the Lord; it is in your hands."

JANUARY 29

"You are an inseparable part of eternity."

DECEMBER 3

"The world has nothing to offer you as far as enlightenment is concerned."

JANUARY 30

"There is nothing higher than Life itself."

DECEMBER 2

"You can postpone everything else, but don't postpone enlightenment."

JANUARY 31

*"You are a luminous soul, a spark of the eternal
fire of Atman."*

DECEMBER 1

"Spirituality dawns when individuality vanishes."

FEBRUARY 1

*"The most ancient language in the world
is the language of love."*

NOVEMBER 30

"The highest practice is to search for Truth through one's thoughts, speech, and actions."

FEBRUARY 2

"The best method of communication is not through the mind or speech; the best communication is through the heart."

NOVEMBER 29

"For those who understand the secret of life, their day-to-day life becomes an act of worship."

FEBRUARY 3

"You can never know your mind without knowing your heart."

NOVEMBER 28

*"The highest worship is beyond rituals and worship of
images. It is inner worship—the direct silent
communication with the divine within."*

FEBRUARY 4

"Mind and heart should become one."

NOVEMBER 27

"Meditation is a mirror in which you see yourself."

FEBRUARY 5

"Love means non-hurting, non-harming, non-injuring, and non-killing, not only through actions, but through speech and thoughts also."

NOVEMBER 26

"Meditation is an inward journey from the external self to the internal Self, the source of consciousness."

FEBRUARY 6

"Every individual is meant to radiate love from individuality to universality."

NOVEMBER 25

"Having no experience in meditation is the right experience."

FEBRUARY 7

"Live in the world and love all, excluding none."

NOVEMBER 24

"When mind starts flowing spontaneously towards its object, that is meditation."

FEBRUARY 8

"One who does not love one's fellow beings cannot love God."

NOVEMBER 23

"Meditation is self-effort, a probe into inner life, and will reveal all the secrets to you in time to come."

FEBRUARY 9

*"You can never hate anyone if you are aware
of one universal consciousness."*

NOVEMBER 22

"The mantra eventually becomes an ocean of bliss in which the mind is floating."

FEBRUARY 10

"Life without love would be an utterly vacant experience."

NOVEMBER 21

"When you remember your mantra, you should remember it with all your feeling."

FEBRUARY 11

*"The Lord of life is love, and that love is eternally
flowing from the Lord of the universe."*

NOVEMBER 20

"Let your mind be led by your mantra and let your mantra become a part of your life."

FEBRUARY 12

"The greatest strength a human being can have is the gentle strength of love."

NOVEMBER 19

"True stillness is not merely the absence of movement; it means to attend effortlessly to your duties without being unduly affected by external circumstances."

FEBRUARY 13

"Strength lies in love, not in violence."

NOVEMBER 18

"The first principle of learning to be still is regular practice, the second is patience, the third is observation, and the fourth is analysis."

FEBRUARY 14

*"Love means to appreciate and enjoy the
divine essence in another person."*

NOVEMBER 17

"Learn to be still and let God reveal Himself to you."

FEBRUARY 15

"Those who want to realize the greatest delight should realize themselves in others."

NOVEMBER 16

"Power is in stillness as much as in movement."

FEBRUARY 16

"Nonattachment and love are the same thing."

NOVEMBER 15

"Meditation is a journey without movement."

FEBRUARY 17

"Real love means letting go of the familiar and the material and leaping into the endless wave of pure love for Truth."

NOVEMBER 14

"Selfless service is the finest of all prayers."

FEBRUARY 18

"Truth is the divine force that dwells in
every individual's heart."

Pic: Dr. Sanjoy Da
Mob: 94111135-

NOVEMBER 13

"Pray in your own language to the Lord of life, who is seated in the inner chamber of your being."

FEBRUARY 19

"Love knows not time, for it is timeless."

NOVEMBER 12

*"Prayer can solve that which cannot be solved
in any other way."*

FEBRUARY 20

*"When you cast off all the fetters of inconsistency
and uncertainty, then alone do you grow in the spirit
of limitless love."*

NOVEMBER 11

*"Prayer and repentance are the greatest purifiers that purify
the way of life and lead us to Self-realization."*

FEBRUARY 21

"Reverence is the first rung on the ladder of love."

NOVEMBER 10

"Prayers are always answered; therefore, pray with all your mind and heart."

FEBRUARY 22

"To love beloved God in any object is knowledge; to understand God in the heart is real Truth."

NOVEMBER 9

*"The joys received through prayer, meditation, and
contemplation are the highest of all joys."*

FEBRUARY 23

*"There is only one perennial flame burning in
the altar of the heart."*

NOVEMBER 8

"If you cannot see God within yourself, what type of God are you looking for in church?"

FEBRUARY 24

*"I have found that in the heart of disappointment
there is always seated a limitless joy that can
emancipate one from sorrow."*

NOVEMBER 7

"Darkness is the distance you create from the center of light."

FEBRUARY 25

"My love is the revelation of the Divinity in me."

NOVEMBER 6

"A true lover of God finds God."

FEBRUARY 26

*"Love for the divine brings one in touch with
one's own divine nature."*

NOVEMBER 5

"Cease this incessant talk about God and seek to meet and know God personally."

FEBRUARY 27

"The power of love is more powerful than any other force."

NOVEMBER 4

"God is all—a personal god, a universal god and that which is beyond."

FEBRUARY 28

"Real love is an inner bond that can never be broken."

NOVEMBER 3

"Do not search for God outside. God is already within you."

FEBRUARY 29

*"One can sing the songs of life, but the songs
of true love are unsung."*

NOVEMBER 2

"Belief in the existence of God indicates that one is searching for the Truth."

MARCH 1

"Philosophy is not love of factual knowledge; it is love of the knowledge of life and the ultimate Reality."

NOVEMBER 1

"To believe in God is not a bad thing."

MARCH 2

*"Human birth is not an accidental phenomenon;
it has a purpose."*

OCTOBER 31

"Where this life ends, the mystery of love begins."

MARCH 3

*"Life is exquisitely perfect the way it drives
people in their evolution."*

OCTOBER 30

"The stream of life flows perennially from eternity to eternity."

MARCH 4

"Out of the tumult of human life comes the decision to look for lasting peace and joy."

OCTOBER 29

*"We are all making a sacred journey to
our true divine nature."*

MARCH 5

*"How could one possibly live fully without
comprehending the meaning of life?"*

OCTOBER 28

"The inner Self does not and cannot die because it is eternal."

MARCH 6

*"Worldly, transitory life, with all of its charms, is
not the purpose of human existence. "*

OCTOBER 27

"The death of the body is not the end of the soul."

MARCH 7

"The goal of life is spiritual."

OCTOBER 26

"Atman is everlasting, unchangeable, and therefore not subject to death."

MARCH 8

"The purpose of life is to grow, expand, and realize one's true identity."

OCTOBER 25

"A flower is a living beauty that blooms only once and vanishes forever."

MARCH 9

"Every human being is born with all the means and resources necessary to attain the goal."

OCTOBER 24

"The wise person sees the futility in the endless pattern of death and rebirth, and looks within for that which is eternal."

MARCH 10

"Dharma is the path a person takes to best use this life to most effectively reach the goal of life."

OCTOBER 23

"Death does not touch the real Self."

MARCH 11

"The paths differ, but the goal is only One."

OCTOBER 22

"This world has come from the silence and ultimately will return to the silence."

MARCH 12

"The goal is to meet God face to face."

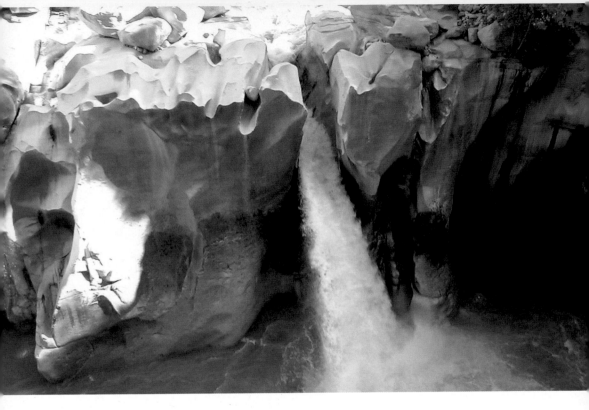

OCTOBER 21

"A soul is like a ripple in the vast ocean of bliss. It comes from the ocean, plays in the ocean, and subsides in the ocean."

MARCH 13

"Nothing in the world can give you happiness."

OCTOBER 20

"Life on this earth is but a brief moment; utilize that moment to purify the way of the soul."

MARCH 14

"The treasure of human life, the real Self, is to be found within."

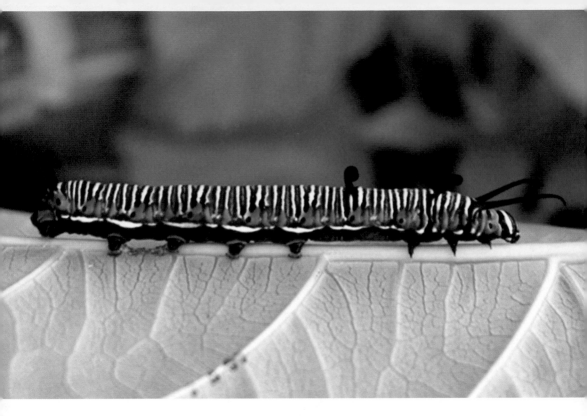

OCTOBER 19

"It is a law of life that in order to step forward, you have to leave behind the ground on which you are standing."

MARCH 15

*"We are like seeds with hard outer coverings,
crying from within for liberation."*

OCTOBER 18

*"Learn to use the things of the world
without being possessive."*

MARCH 16

"The soul does not need to be cured or healed; it seeks only to be experienced and known."

OCTOBER 17

"Death reminds you not to attach yourself to this world."

MARCH 17

"Wake up, remain awake and gain the knowledge that can liberate you."

OCTOBER 16

"All worldly pleasures are limited by time."

MARCH 18

"Peace cannot be attained through mere speculative philosophy or logic."

OCTOBER 15

"Behind every pleasure is pain, behind every expectation is disappointment, and following every fulfilled desire is yet another desire."

MARCH 19

*"Inner freedom is born from self-sacrifice,
self-purification, and self-control."*

OCTOBER 14

"The body is no more a person's identity than the reflection of the sun on the surface of a calm lake is the real sun."

MARCH 20

*"A human being is a citizen of two worlds, the
world within and the world outside."*

OCTOBER 13

"The greatest obstacle in the path of realization is attachment to the body and the objects of the world."

MARCH 21

*"The world within and the world without are
two entirely separate realities."*

OCTOBER 12

"People cling to their desires till death and drag them all back with them again to the worldly plane where they can be fulfilled."

MARCH 22

*"The purpose of life is to attain a state of
freedom from all misery and pain."*

OCTOBER 11

"When you leave this world you carry all of your experiences with you in the unconscious mind."

MARCH 23

"Ignorance is the root cause of all pain, misery, and suffering."

OCTOBER 10

*"Anyone who becomes attached to the phenomenal world with
all of its changing forms is sure to come to grief in the end."*

MARCH 24

"All suffering comes from lack of self-realization."

OCTOBER 9

"The phenomenal universe is impermanent and is constantly changing, evolving, growing, decaying, and dying."

MARCH 25

"Self-realization comes only when you are fully prepared."

OCTOBER 8

"All of life's events try to teach that out of death comes life."

MARCH 26

*"There is a center of consciousness beyond mind
and that is your individual soul."*

OCTOBER 7

"We remain in the known for only a short time, but the unknown is always with us."

MARCH 27

"From the center of consciousness flows the life force on various degrees and grades."

OCTOBER 6

*"We have come from the unknown and we will
return to the unknown."*

MARCH 28

"Enlightenment is expansion of consciousness."

OCTOBER 5

"Life is a long procession from the unknown to the unknown."

MARCH 29

*"When consciousness expands, pain vanishes,
and eternal joy appears."*

OCTOBER 4

"Death is not a period, but merely a pause on a long journey."

MARCH 30

"Freedom is a divine gift lent to mortals."

OCTOBER 3

"Death and birth seem to be an unending cycle."

MARCH 31

"Spirituality has infinite horizons and limitless freedom."

OCTOBER 2

"You are an ancient traveler who keeps coming and going in this world."

APRIL 1

"Life is a manuscript, and you are the author of that manuscript."

OCTOBER 1

"Life is brief and precious."

APRIL 2

"You are not as small as you think you are."

SEPTEMBER 30

"The whole essence of discipline is wrapped inside a small thing called love."

APRIL 3

"Even if you go to the end of the world to search for yourself, you will never meet anyone like you."

SEPTEMBER 29

"If you practice, you will experience, and that experience will guide you."

APRIL 4

"As a human being, deep within, you are perfect and complete."

SEPTEMBER 28

"Lord, let me not stumble on the path of Truth."

APRIL 5

"Your inner world is larger and more powerful than the world around you. There is something great inside you."

SEPTEMBER 27

"The path of Truth is narrower than the needle's eye and as sharp as a razor's edge."

APRIL 6

*"The Lord is within you, seated deep beyond
your mind and emotions."*

SEPTEMBER 26

"To be spiritual means to be aware of the Reality all the time."

APRIL 7

"The day you come to know that the Lord is within, you will be free from fear."

SEPTEMBER 25

"Surrender the mind for a while to God consciousness, and you will find peace."

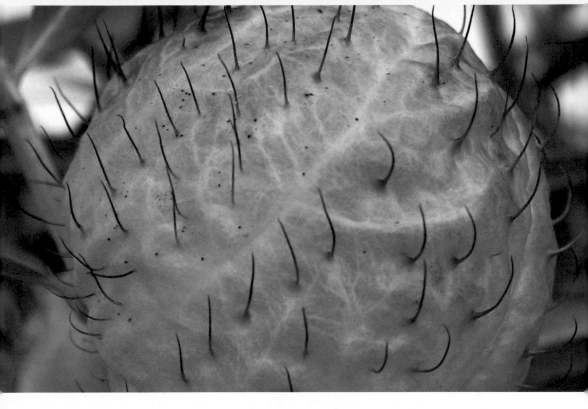

APRIL 8

"The potential to realize the Truth is present in every person."

SEPTEMBER 24

"Let yourself become a willing instrument."

APRIL 9

*"Truth is that which remains unchanged
in past, present, and future."*

SEPTEMBER 23

*"The first step toward enlightenment is to learn
to follow the conscience and not the mind."*

APRIL 10

*"Those who remain on the thinking level do not get
the opportunity to see what they are within."*

SEPTEMBER 22

"No matter who you are, whether a swami or an ordinary person living in the world, you should learn the technique of living in the world yet remaining unaffected."

APRIL 11

"The conscious mind fails to grasp that which lies beyond the spheres of time, space, and causation."

SEPTEMBER 21

"Learn to be strong from within."

APRIL 12

"Mind is an obstacle for the ignorant, and a means for the wise."

SEPTEMBER 20

"If you do not have faith in yourself, how can you have faith in God?"

APRIL 13

"Mind has immense potential."

SEPTEMBER 19

"True belief, or faith, comes after direct experience."

APRIL 14

"You must change your worldview and start looking at life from another perspective."

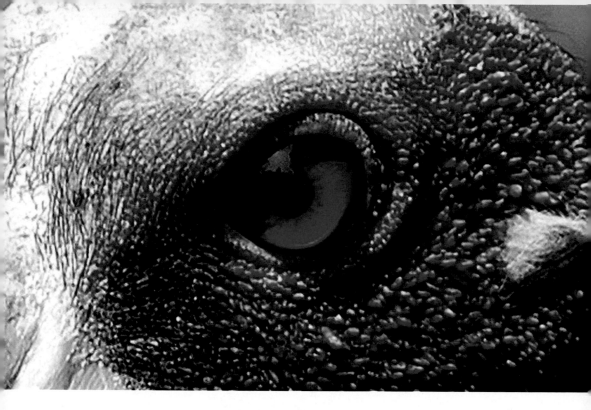

SEPTEMBER 18

"Blind faith is always subject to scrutiny."

APRIL 15

"Creativity and discovery lie beyond the mind."

SEPTEMBER 17

"The realm of faith creates perfection."

APRIL 16

"You are a pure soul—that is your real nature."

SEPTEMBER 16

"Faith in God leads one to God."

APRIL 17

"The soul is that which is beyond mind and personality;
it is your essential nature."

SEPTEMBER 15

"Patience is a great virtue that needs to be cultivated."

APRIL 18

*"A human being has within all the resources needed
to attain the highest state of wisdom."*

SEPTEMBER 14

"Increase your capacity slowly and gradually;
learn to be patient with yourself."

APRIL 19

"You have all the knowledge within, but you have to make effort to come in touch with that knowledge."

SEPTEMBER 13

"Be confident and self-reliant and say to yourself,
'I will do it. I can do it. I have to do it.'"

APRIL 20

"In life everything does not happen the way you want it to happen."

SEPTEMBER 12

"You should never give up working with yourself."

APRIL 21

"It is possible to live perfectly on earth if one is able to work and to love—to work for what one loves, and to love what one is working at."

SEPTEMBER 11

"Sliding backward is part of the pattern of growth."

Pic: Dr Sanjoy Da

APRIL 22

"By living fully in the world with all of its apparent imperfections one can attain spiritual perfection."

SEPTEMBER 10

"Determination is the power that sees us through all frustrations and obstacles."

APRIL 23

"There is something beyond the realm of knowing.
That something is called silence."

SEPTEMBER 9

"Decide that no matter what happens, you will do what you set out to do."

APRIL 24

"Everlasting happiness is within."

SEPTEMBER 8

"Discipline means self-commitment."

APRIL 25

"Each individual is a wave in the single vast ocean of pure consciousness."

SEPTEMBER 7

"To attain perfection here and now, you must undertake some spiritual discipline."

APRIL 26

"You can be liberated right here and now."

SEPTEMBER 6

"Practice, not mere theory, will make you perfect."

APRIL 27

"Confidence comes when you go to the source that is the immortal part of your being."

SEPTEMBER 5

*"All sadhanas, all practices, are meant to
purify and strengthen the mind."*

APRIL 28

*"Who can there be more wonderful than my Self—
that is the Self of all?"*

Pic: Dr. Sanjoy Das

SEPTEMBER 4

"The greatest of all sins is sloth."

APRIL 29

"No god is greater than thy Self."

SEPTEMBER 3

*"You really do not need to know many things, but
you definitely need to practice what you know."*

APRIL 30

"The time will come when you will know all that is to be known."

SEPTEMBER 2

*"There are many barriers to cross before you reach the
fountainhead of life and light within."*

MAY 1

"A mother has more responsibility than any other person, and that responsibility should be enjoyed, rather than carried as a burden."

SEPTEMBER 1

"Be gentle with yourself. This is a long and difficult journey."

MAY 2

"Women have a hidden power that men can never fully understand."

AUGUST 31

"Love will completely transform you, for love alone has that power."

MAY 3

"What our society needs today is men and women who realize the importance of creating healthy families."

AUGUST 30

"Remember the Lord all the time and sooner or later you will be transformed."

MAY 4

"The foundation for life is established in childhood, especially in the first seven years."

AUGUST 29

"Grace dawns when you have completed your human efforts."

MAY 5

"There is no better foundation for a happy life
than a happy childhood."

AUGUST 28

"Learn to identify with the source of light and life."

MAY 6

"Children are only children; they need to be trained, but they should always be treated with affection and respect."

AUGUST 27

"Only a pure mind can attain one-pointedness."

MAY 7

"A child can teach you what love is."

AUGUST 26

"Self-transformation is possible through meditation."

MAY 8

"If you want to see the image of the living God, you can see it in the faces of children."

AUGUST 25

"Death has no power to change you, but you have
the power to transform yourself."

MAY 9

"For a person who has the capacity to love and see the divine within, the greatest joy in the world is a child."

AUGUST 24

"If you have an aim or purpose in life, you can bring your emotional life under control."

MAY 10

*"Marriage is like a cart with two wheels. Each wheel
helps the other to roll along the path."*

AUGUST 23

*"People who know how to use their emotions creatively become
successful in the external world and remain happy."*

MAY 11

"Marriage is a commitment that must be made with one's full heart and mind."

AUGUST 22

"Every form has an idea behind it, and every idea has a desire behind it."

MAY 12

"Emotion means relationship, and relationship means life. As long as you do not participate in life you will remain lonely."

AUGUST 21

"All desires arise from four primitive fountains: self-preservation, sleep, food, and sex."

MAY 13

*"Relationships become very easy if you understand
each other and accept each other as you are; then
you can help each other."*

AUGUST 20

"The root cause of all emotions is desire."

MAY 14

"The path of loving relationships is the path of the heart, rather than the path of the mind or intellect."

AUGUST 19

"The emotional level is deeper than the level of thoughts."

MAY 15

"Adjustment leads to contentment."

AUGUST 18

"The emotional body is like a fish tossed by the currents in the lake of the mind."

Pic: Dr. Sanjoy
Mob: 941111
Email: visitdas@rediffmai

MAY 16

"Forgiveness is the greatest of all virtues."

AUGUST 17

"All your actions are controlled by your thoughts, and all your thoughts are controlled by your emotions."

MAY 17

"The highest guiding principle in marriage should be the principle of selfless service to one's partner."

AUGUST 16

*"It is the nature of mind to flow in the grooves
of past experiences."*

MAY 18

"The more selfish you are, the more you will suffer in life."

AUGUST 15

"In order to make spiritual progress, you need to first understand your thinking process."

MAY 19

"Every human being has something to offer to others."

AUGUST 14

"You can live in the world and yet be spiritual. It is not necessary for you to renounce the world."

MAY 20

"As life is to live, love is to give."

AUGUST 13

*"We all know what to do and what not to do, but it
is very difficult to know how to be."*

MAY 21

"It is good to have the goal of universal love, but first, you should learn to love those who are closest to you."

AUGUST 12

*"When you open the real eye within,
you will see things as they are."*

MAY 22

"Learn to love others and demonstrate your love through selfless action."

AUGUST 11

"If you continue to build castles in the sky, the psychiatrist will collect the rent."

MAY 23

"Selflessness is the singular expression of love."

AUGUST 10

"You see things as you want to see them, not as they are."

MAY 24

*"Learn to express yourself in such a way that you
don't hurt, injure, or harm others."*

AUGUST 9

"Your mind is the wall that stands between you and the Reality."

MAY 25

*"Express yourself with all the gentleness that you can,
for gentleness and love are one and the same."*

AUGUST 8

"You only have to change your attitude toward life and the world; you have not to change yourself."

MAY 26

"Do your duties in the world with love."

AUGUST 7

"You are the sum total of your habits."

MAY 27

"Nothing can change human destiny but love."

AUGUST 6

"The process of transformation requires regularity and vigilance."

MAY 28

*"All human beings are different, but all inhale
and exhale the same life force."*

AUGUST 5

"Transformation is not change; transformation is growth."

MAY 29

"Unless we learn to become aware of others and we are sensitive to them, we can never fully develop as human beings."

AUGUST 4

"*Once you turn your focus inward, the process of transformation will begin; then you will become aware of the many levels of consciousness.*"

MAY 30

*"The more we do for others, the more we discover
the secret of love."*

AUGUST 3

"You can definitely improve and grow once you become aware of the fact that you are fully responsible for your actions."

MAY 31

"Love does not question, expect a reward, or doubt."

AUGUST 2

"If you really want to know who you are, you have to take off all the masks, one after the other."

JUNE 1

"The basis of holistic health lies in understanding the purpose of life and learning how to achieve that purpose."

AUGUST 1

"You have to take responsibility for your own life."

JUNE 2

"Physical health is considered to be an essential part of spiritual practice."

JULY 31

"You have to light your own lamp."

JUNE 3

"Only after you have learned to take care of the body can you tread the path of inner life."

JULY 30

"As long as you doubt, it means you have yet to know."

JUNE 4

"Body is a projection of mind."

JULY 29

*"Direct experience is the highest of all means
to gain knowledge."*

JUNE 5

"All of the body is in the mind, but all of the mind is not in the body."

JULY 28

"Guru sustains, nurtures, and guides a soul through lifetimes to ultimate liberation."

JUNE 6

"Most diseases are self-created."

JULY 27

"Only if you prepare yourself will you deserve to receive the higher knowledge."

JUNE 7

*"You can create many diseases through your own mind
and you can heal yourself through the same mind."*

JULY 26

"Deserve first and then desire."

JUNE 8

"One should cultivate and practice those skills that ensure health, rather than fall victim to those that perpetuate disease."

JULY 25

"Shaktipata is only possible when the disciple has gone through a long period of discipline, austerity, and spiritual practice."

JUNE 9

"The nature of inner life changes the quality of external life."

JULY 24

"Self-discipline can be achieved only through the conscious directing of your will."

JUNE 10

"When mind is disturbed, your biochemistry changes."

JULY 23

"Those who do not believe in discipline should not expect enlightenment."

JUNE 11

*"Any unrest in the body and nervous system
is because of the mind."*

JULY 22

*"Shaktipata is the grace of God transmitted
through the master."*

JUNE 12

"The breath is the bridge between body and mind."

JULY 21

"Guru is a force that helps to move a soul toward enlightenment."

JUNE 13

"Proper breathing is the key to good health."

JULY 20

"As the sun shines and remains far above, the guru gives spiritual love and remains unattached."

JUNE 14

"Life is breath and breath is life."

JULY 19

"Ego is that which separates you from the Reality, the Truth, and the ultimate Source."

JUNE 15

"Attitude is the most important factor in realizing health."

JULY 18

"The final barrier is ego."

JUNE 16

"Worrying is a disease that you have acquired."

JULY 17

"The only strength a person can rely on is inner strength, and that inner strength is based on love."

JUNE 17

"Cheerfulness is the greatest of all physicians."

JULY 16

*"Faith and determination are two essential rungs
on the ladder of enlightenment."*

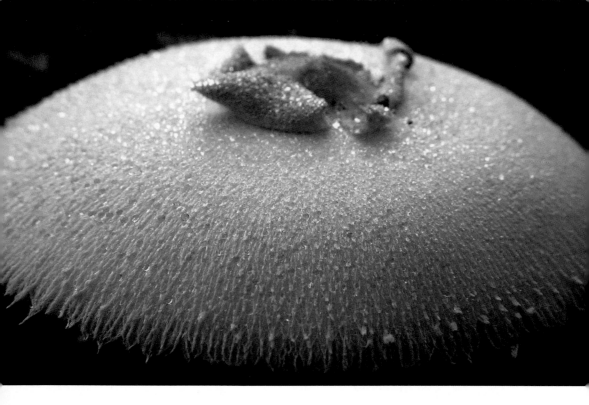

JUNE 18

"Contentment is the greatest wealth you could ever have."

JULY 15

*"The most important teachings have their source in intuition
and are beyond the powers of verbal communication."*

JUNE 19

"Happiness is not having what you want, but wanting what you have."

JULY 14

"Guru is a tradition, a stream of knowledge."

JUNE 20

"If you want to live positively and joyfully, give the fruits of your actions to others and determine that you will not allow yourself to be bothered by anything in the external world."

JULY 13

"You have to put gold in the fire in order for it to shine."

JUNE 21

"Enjoy life from moment to moment and do not get disturbed."

JULY 12

"What I realize is that the life force is upon me to do what God wants, and not what I want."

JUNE 22

"There is no conflict in life. Conflict lies in the mind."

JULY 11

*"The thoughts, speech, and actions of an illumined
person are in perfect harmony."*

JUNE 23

"If something does not turn favorable in life, one should learn to forget and start a fresh chapter."

JULY 10

"Guru is a channel for spiritual knowledge."

JUNE 24

"Loneliness is the root cause of many diseases."

JULY 9

"With the help of sankalpa shakti, the power of determination, nothing is impossible."

JUNE 25

"People are lonely because they are not aware
of the fountain within."

JULY 8

"Spiritual desire consumes all trivial desires and attachments."

JUNE 26

"The mental aspect of health is more important than the physical, and the spiritual aspect is of greater importance than either of these."

JULY 7

"Grace is the result of sincere effort."

JUNE 27

*"Self-accepted discipline helps to keep the body
healthy and the mind sound."*

JULY 6

"The greatest power in the world is the divine power of grace."

JUNE 28

"Learn to flow with life and all of its ups and downs."

JULY 5

"The purpose of a guide, guru, or teacher is to introduce you to that light."

JUNE 29

"Meditational therapy is the highest of all therapies."

JULY 4

"Go to the inner levels of your being and be guided by the light that is already within you."

JUNE 30

"Every human life contains the power for self-healing."

JULY 3

"Search for the guru within yourself."

JULY 1

*"On the path of spirituality there is always
guidance from the unknown."*

JULY 2

"That which dispels the darkness of ignorance is called guru."

SWAMI RAMA

A disciple of the Himalayan adept, Sri Bengali Baba, Swami Rama was born and raised in the Garhwal region of the Himalayas. A highly accomplished yogi, teacher, scientist, philosopher, humanitarian, and writer, he dedicated his life to serving humanity. For more than 25 years he lectured throughout the world in monasteries, churches, universities, and medical schools. His models of preventive medicine, holistic health and stress management have permeated the mainstream of western medicine.

Swamiji was also the author of many books. His contributions to literature include profound commentaries on such spiritual works as the Bhagavad Gita and the Upanishads; practical guidelines to the application of the ancient wisdom of the East to the field of psychology and health; a poetic rendition of the Valmiki Ramayana; an inspiring account of his experiences with the great teachers who guided his life and spiritual development; and a deeply personal collection of prose poetry of his own spiritual experiences.

In order to serve the underprivileged population of his beloved Garhwal, Swamiji founded the Himalayan Institute Hospital Trust near Dehradun. From a small outpatient clinic that opened in 1989, the Trust has grown into a huge medical city and deemed university that incorporates an ultra modern 1000-bed hospital, a medical college, a college of nursing, a rural development institute and a large cancer institute soon to be completed.

Swamiji's deep love for his ancient spiritual tradition was reflected in his life and work. He was a free thinker, guided by direct experience and inner wisdom. His life embodied the human potential to live in the world, yet remain above.

The beautiful photographs included in this perpetual calendar echo the divine nature of Swamiji's inspiring sayings that have been gathered from the vast volume of his books and lectures, to remind us to seek within.